To Jack
with love

Mary R

Aug 20, 1976

ENGLISH SPORTING GUNS
AND ACCESSORIES

Frontispiece: **The beautiful coloured engraving of partridge shooting, reproduced here by courtesy of Messrs. Arthur Ackermann & Son, of 3 Old Bond Street, is one of a series of twenty, after designs by Samuel Howitt (*c*.1760–1822), published by E. Orme of Bond Street in 1807–1808. The two sportsmen are shooting what appear to be single-barrelled full-stocked flintlocks. The dogs are pointers, the most popular sporting dog of the period. The month, from the foliage on the trees, must be September. The partridge manor, from the pattern of the landscape and its buildings, probably took its inspiration from the water meadows of Hampshire. Note how on charge the old muzzleloading guns spout clouds of smoke from both ends of the barrels. Modern photographs of the phenomenon are on pages 8–9. The unbalanced stance and grip of the shooters is discussed on pages 19–21.**

ENGLISH
SPORTING GUNS
AND ACCESSORIES

Macdonald Hastings

WARD LOCK & COMPANY LIMITED
LONDON AND SYDNEY

Books on Guns and Shooting by the same Author

CHURCHILL ON GAME SHOOTING
(In collaboration with Robert Churchill)

THE OTHER MR. CHURCHILL
(Biography)

HOW TO SHOOT STRAIGHT
(For newcomers to the shooting field)

© Macdonald Hastings 1969
7063 1053 5

Printed in Great Britain by Cox & Wyman Limited
London · Reading · Fakenham
Set in Monotype Times

THIS monograph is an introduction to English Sporting Guns from the end of the eighteenth century to the second half of the nineteenth when breechloaders came into general use. It dates from the period when sportsmen went shooting in a pot hat to the time when they adopted deerstalkers and Highland tweeds.

I have limited my comments to guns and accessories which if proper precautions are taken can be used in the field today. Although I admit to shooting brancher rooks with a duelling pistol, slaughtering flocks of sparrows with a coach guard's blunderbuss, they are not the conventional weapons of sport. I have consequently left them out.

I have dealt only briefly with rifled arms and airguns, interesting specialities as they are for the collector. The reason is that Britain, outside the Highlands of Scotland, is primarily a shotgun country. Airguns and air rifles, wrongly as it happens, are usually designated boy's guns; and, when it comes to the things euphemistically termed 'Naturalist's Canes', they are correctly defined as poachers' weapons.

Neither have I discussed large bore fowling pieces, stanchion or punt guns. Beloved of the Victorians, hardly anybody uses cannon of that sort today; and a collector would need a museum to house them.

I have written not simply in terms of lock, stock and barrel; but of the people who used these old arms, and how.

To the dedicated collector there is more fun in some rusty old game gun, or dented powder flask, when he also has a knowledge of the period when the gun first bellowed and smoked over the stubbles and the marshes. Nothing is more exciting than to discern, out of collector's detective work, whose were the initials, whose the monogram on an old gun-case or gunstock; few games are more entertaining than to puzzle out what all the strange accessories the nineteenth century gunmakers provided were meant to do.

So much of the enchantment of collecting old arms, and the furnishing that goes with them, is in discovery. I remember that in the bad old days of the war after Dunkirk an appeal was made to America to send weapons, any weapons, to equip the newly-formed Home Guard. All manner of fire irons were sent by willing souls across the Atlantic. It happened that I was deputed to look over the stuff. I found a 12-bore gun which, on a gold plate on the stock, carried the inscription: 'To Annie Oakley, Little Sure Shot, from William Greener.' Annie Oakley was the crack-shot of Buffalo Bill's Wild West Show. William Greener was one of the famous English gunmakers of his day.

You might pick up an arm of that sort for a song even now from somebody who doesn't know its worth, or its origins. But it is becoming increasingly difficult. You might have a little bit of luck with a find in an attic, or a gun you have identified on an inn wall. But you can congratulate yourself these days if a snip comes your way. You have only to attend one of the regular antique arms auctions, up and down the country, to learn current values in the open market.

Faraway, I remember buying a pair of duelling pistols from a junk shop in a court off Fleet Street for one pound. At the time it seemed a lot of money. I sold the pair at auction recently for two hundred and forty guineas.

Back in the thirties there was no interest at all, except among a dedicated few, in vintage weapons. You could buy them at the price of second hand pokers. Some did. Gunmakers' shops were glad to give old stock away.

At the risk of being argued with, I date the beginnings of

the change, from disinterest to enthusiasm, from the first publication of Major Hugh B. C. Pollard's *History of Firearms* in 1923. It was a pioneer effort based almost entirely on the author's original research. The work, not surprisingly, is now in many respects out of date; although still a valuable one for the bibliophile. The boom began, as booms so often do, in the United States. In the search for a hunting novelty, or upmanship in house decoration, the muzzleloaders came into their own again.

So while I have primarily addressed myself here to collectors with a taste for reliving the field conditions of the past, it is worth noting that anyone who buys antique arms and accessories, wisely and well, can nowadays count on making a profit on the investment.

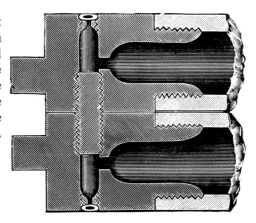

Henry Nock's historic patent (No. 1598, April 25, 1787) in which the touch hole is pierced into a chamber in the centre of the breech-plug. Thus the priming powder ignites the middle of the charge in the barrel.

1787–1900

It is unlikely that the collector will come upon any sporting arm in shootable condition built earlier than the last decade of the eighteenth century. Whatever its outward appearance it would in any event be hazardous to subject a barrel of an earlier age to the pressures of powder and shot.*

The most venerable weapon I have fired is the Henry Nock

---

* *There are exceptions. Mr. Keith Neal, the distinguished collector, fires a wheellock. Guns of the seventeenth and eighteenth century can be found in shootable condition; but only an expert should venture in the use of them.*

7

gun (page 38) which is also the earliest weapon I have illustrated. It is cautionary to mention that, after a few shots with a nominal charge, the gold disc over the touch hole flew off, the bead of the foresight tumbled in sheer exhaustion, and I was lucky that the barrel didn't disintegrate in my hands. Anyhow it is a poor piece which, at sometime in the past, some blacksmith has interfered with.

But Nock's gun – the lock (page 42) is as beautiful as ever – is an appropriate one for a start because it incorporates his 'Patent Breech', a matter duly recorded on a gold shield – more correctly a poinçon – on the barrel. Anybody who studies nineteenth century sporting arms soon recognizes that patents of one sort or another were at that time two a penny. Most of the patents claimed by rivalling gunmakers in a period of swift change, were transitory and insignificant.

Henry Nock of London, with his patent of April, 1787, achieved a breakthrough. Prior to his patent, the plug at the base of the barrel of a muzzleloading gun was a solid lump of

Compare what is depicted in the sporting prints
with the truth of shooting with a muzzleloader.
This sequence of photographs shows how, after
fire, the shooter is blinded by a pall of smoke.
With modern black powder the picture is perhaps clearer
but still too fogged for the shooter to be
sure that he is on target.

metal.* What this meant was that, when the flint sparked the powder in the pan, the flame spurting into the touchhole ignited only a corner of the charge in the barrel. As a consequence, it took longer for the powder to burn. In Nock's gun, the touchhole was pierced into a chamber in the centre of the plug with the result that the priming powder fired the middle of the charge. Guns shot harder and quicker.

After nearly two hundred years of comparative stagnancy in gun design, from the time when the flintlock superseded the matchlock, the wheellock and the snaphaunce, it was from Nock's patent that the gun invention leapt forward. The immediate result of it, ensuring quicker burning of powder, was that it became possible to make an effective reduction of

Not strictly true. Chambered guns were produced prior to Nock's patent; but his was the successful one. Collectors who wish to study the matter in detail are commended to the bibliography. My own aim is to express myself as briefly as possible in correct, if not fully detailed, terms. Precision is impossible to achieve in a small compass, without confounding the reader, in the maze of nineteenth century gunmaking.

**It is always difficult to sight the second barrel.
On a windless day the only hope is to look for a
crossing or away shot. The remarkable performances
of the top game shots in the last half of the
nineteenth century can be attributed, in part if
not in whole, to the introduction of smokeless powders.**

gun barrels from about 40-inches to 30-inches; to encourage better balanced half stocked weapons with the weight of metal in the middle; and to open the way for double barrelled guns. At last, shooting was not a matter of creeping in for a raking shot at low range; but a sport. From Nock's time the way was open, from the clumsy long-barrelled weapons of Queen Anne's reign – the sort of weapon carried by the eighteenth century gamekeeper on page 32 – to the evolution of the breechloader.

Within a few years change was so rapid that it is no wonder that the nineteenth century gunmakers produced a new patent every few years, or months. Bemused sportsmen had their guns changed again and again to bring them up to date with the latest invention. The result is that not the least of the collector's problems today is to distinguish between guns which have subsequently been faked or renovated, and guns which were converted, perhaps by the original maker, from flint to percussion, and even to work with both systems.

To get a grasp of a complex phase of firearms development, it is useful to have a tabulation of dates. The collector should remember that the introduction of a new device did not mean that it was popularly accepted. On the contrary, it is safe to say that it was generally opposed. It was many years before Colonel Peter Hawker, 'the father of game shooting', conceded that percussion was better than flint. He had private doubts about it up to his death in the fifties.

Sporting men have always been a conservative breed. Lord Walsingham, named in Victorian times as one of 'the ten best shots in England', dismissed the introduction of Whitworth steel barrels because he didn't like the noise the charge made going up the spout. I have handled a pair of percussion guns made by a contemporary gunmaker for an eccentric who thought he preferred them to breechloaders. Incidentally, he was disappointed with the replicas. The barrelmaker, no doubt a master of modern choke boring, had never learnt the tricks of making a cylindered muzzleloader.

We have lost, as we have gained, out of the past. Old muzzleloaders – although they take longer to charge, and require

EXTRACT FROM COLONEL PETER HAWKER'S DIARY
(September 17, 1827);
'Assembled my myrmidons for one more grand field day, in order
to have some of their likenesses. Mr. Childe (the artist)
attended as a strict observer, and Mr. Joseph Manton shot
with me. Our united bag was **48** partridges and **1** hare, and
we returned some time before the day was over, in order that
Mr. Childe might complete by good daylight the necessary
sketches of the group. My share of the bag was **28** partridges,
but had I shot entirely by myself, and been able to waive
the usual ceremony of shooting in company, and galloped up
to all my birds, as heretofore, I am confident I should have
killed **30** brace of birds.' (In the engraving, Hawker is on horseback
and Joseph Manton, the great gunmaker, is standing beside him.)

more knowledge in the handling than breechloading arms –
shoot as far and as straight as contemporary weapons. The
evolution of the sporting gun in England during the nineteenth
century is one of the wonders of that remarkable age. It is a
good way to begin to get the essential dates right.

Two significant developments, apart from Nock's Patent
Breeching, sparked the way in the latter half of the eighteenth
century to the explosive invention that followed. In 1782
(Patent No. 1347), William Watts, a Bristol plumber, dis-

covered how to make drop shot. It is said that the notion of
spilling molten lead into water through a sieve from a height so
that it formed like a raindrop came to him in a dream. Before
then shot was cut out of strips into dice and rattled into rough
spheres.

In 1815, Sir William Congreve, Comptroller of the Royal
Laboratory at Woolwich, took out a patent (No. 3937) to
standardize powder. For the first time, gunpowder achieved
calculable efficiency. From that triple start the way was clear.
The pattern, henceforward, plates in this fashion.

1806:   *JOSEPH MANTON'S ELEVATING RIB*
Joseph Manton (1795–1835) was probably the
most inventive London gunmaker of the early
nineteenth century; although he may not have
been the greatest, as Colonel Peter Hawker
insisted that he was. His elevating rib was simply
a raising of the metal bar at the chambers' end
tapering off to the muzzle between the barrels of a
double gun. It was widely acclaimed because it
had the effect of correcting the common error of
shooting low (page 46). Robert Churchill, the
modern gunmaker, incorporated a similar type
rib in his 25-inch barrelled guns to overcome the
fault of shooting behind.

1800–1820: *VINTAGE YEARS OF THE FLINT GUN*
The two decades in which the London gunmakers, led by such as Joseph (1795–1835) and
John Manton (1780–1834), Henry Nock (1772–
1804), Durs Egg (1785–1834) and James Purdey
the first (1816–1835) brought the flint gun to its
highest degree of perfection. The essential shapes
they arrived at are unchanged in breechloaders
today.

1807:   *FIRST DETONATING LOCK*
The invention of a Scottish clergyman, the Rev.

The gunmaker W. W. Greener (1910) describes this as the Correct Position for charging a muzzleloading arm. It isn't. The heel of the gun should be pressed against the boot. The shooter should extend his left arm to get his face out of the way of the barrel.

Alexander James Forsyth, which within a few years made the flint and steel method of ignition obsolete. A fulminate was exploded by the blow of a plunger which instantaneously fired the charge. (Page 48)

1813:   *FIRST GUN BARREL PROOF ACT*

1816–1818: PELLET, CAP AND COPPER TUBE GUNS
Following Forsyth's patent, various detonating devices were developed, including Joseph Manton's percussion tube lock in 1818. The detonating system culminated in the universal use of copper caps mounted on a nipple. (Page 48)

1818–1820: DUAL LOCK SYSTEMS
Before copper caps were standardized to suit all guns, there was an interregnum in which weapons were designed to fire with flint and steel, percussion caps, and even Manton pellet-locks. A particularly confusing, but interesting, half-way house for the collector. Most conversions from

WADS; The old gunners used cut
cork: or, if they weren't particular,
a bit out of the tail of
an old woollen shirt. An oiled wad,
for the overpowder charge, is best.

SHOT; Shot is now standard.
Don't be misled by writers in
the past, like General Hanger,
who recommended No. 3 for
partridges. Stick to No. 5 or 6.

CAPS; The early percussion caps
were so unreliable that Eley
Bros. felt it necessary to
advertise on the tins that 'they
were warranted not to miss-fire
nor fly to pieces.'

FLINTS; It is said that both
sides in the field at Waterloo
fought with Brandon flints. Gun
flints are still knapped in
Suffolk, although it is difficult
now to get the hard ones.

14

PRIMERS, DETONATORS & CONCENTRATORS
Hardware of the latter days of the muzzleloaders, early days of
the breechloaders. The minutiae of percussion cap designs and
tube detonators are revelations of a period of continuous
innovation. The Lancaster concentrators (*above*) were simply sleeves
(like the wire cartridge) to improve the patterning of cylinder
guns before the discovery of choke-boring: the caps in the final stage
before the coming of centre-fire ammunition.

flintlock to percussion proper were made in the
next decade.

1818:   *INTRODUCTION OF DAMASCUS BARRELS*
The gunmaker Rigby of Dublin, made the first
'Damascus' barrels; but they did not come into
general use until after 1825. Prior to that, barrels
were twisted out of horse shoe nail stubs. Damascus barrels (only remotely to do with the place

15

called Damascus) were worked into their beautiful herring-bone patterns by the mingling of iron and steel. Even the new barrels were only reluctantly accepted by the old sportsmen.

1840's: *NEEDLE AND PINFIRE ARMS*
The last short phase before the standardization of the breechloader. The needle and the pin exploded the fulminate inside a cartridge.

1850: *BEGINNING OF THE BREECHLOADER*
The breechloader has earlier origins, but its definite phase was the introduction in France of LeFaucheux's drop down action pinfire with a forward underlever below the fore-end. It was brought to London by the gunmaker Joseph Lang of Cockspur Street in 1851. (Page 56)

1852: *FIRST CARTRIDGE EXTRACTING GUN*
Charles Lancaster brought out a central fire underlever gun with extractors. (Page 57)

1858: *BREECHLOADER ACCEPTED*
Gun trials, organized by *The Field*, settled controversy about the merits, or otherwise, of the breechloading gun, which came into general use in the sixties. Stability in the design of hammer guns was achieved between 1866–1875.

1861: *CENTRAL FIRE CARTRIDGES*
The first true central fire cartridge in Britain was exhibited by Daw of Threadneedle Street at the Great Exhibition of that year. (Page 67)

1866: *CHOKE BORING*
The invention of the choke bore is generally attributed to Pape of Newcastle. W. W. Greener of Birmingham challenged it (1875).

1870:   *PURDEY'S BOLT ACTION*
The son of Purdey the first brought out the familiar slide and top lever arrangement we know today. (Page 60)

1871:   *HAMMERLESS GUNS*
Murcott of Haymarket, introduced the true hammerless gun ('Murcott's mouse trap'). (Page 62)

1875:   *ANSON & DEELEY'S BOX LOCK ACTION*
Two Birmingham craftsmen (of Westley Richards) introduced the simplest, cheapest and, with only three working parts, still one of the most reliable gun actions. (Pages 64–65)

1875:   *SELF-EJECTING GUNS*
Needham, a Birmingham gunsmith, produced the first mechanism to flip a fired cartridge out of a shotgun barrel. Frail and unreliable in the original invention, the system was perfected in the last decade of the century.

1878-1882: *SMOKELESS POWDERS SUCCEEDED BLACK POWDER*

1890:   *PROOF FOR SMOKELESS POWDERS (NITRO POWDERS) COMPULSORY*

1900:   *QUICK RELIABLE SMOKELESS POWDERS*

SHOOTING IN A POT HAT

To make an absolute assertion on any matter appertaining to gun performance and sporting practice in England until about the last quarter of the nineteenth century, as the new collector will soon discover, is simply an invitation to a more experienced one to adduce evidence to shoot it down. So much is controversial. After all, we don't know for certain, nor ever

17

Colonel Peter Hawker (1786–1853) who represents the first school of gameshooting, was succeeded by Victorians who, with the aid of the breechloader and smokeless powders, brought the sport to formidable efficiency. By the eighties, a code of conduct in the field was established. Huge bags were made, of a size that Hawker never imagined. The rules of shooting safely in line were firmly agreed.

THE RIGHT SORT

will, who in the dark past discovered powder and cannon. After less than a hundred and fifty years, he is a bold man who claims to know all the wrinkles which came naturally to the pot-hatted characters in the pastoral world of the sporting prints.

The weapons, the accessories they used, are still with us. They left behind them a large and fascinating literature; but the more closely you read it the more the feeling grows that they didn't put down things that to them, in their stilted prose, usually littered with classical tags, seemed obvious. I am increasingly convinced that they had a know-how which enabled them to shoot better than any of us using their old guns, with superior black powder and regular shot, can achieve today.

Major Hugh Pollard used to instruct me that the best approach to antique arms is the application of common sense. It is more likely to lead to a correct solution than the small print of an old book. In brief it is better to make a guess; and, at the expense of a pun, to chance your arm.*

---

* Not in the field. In the next section I have discussed the safety precautions which are necessary before muzzleloaders are brought to life again.

18

**For a date gameshooting, as it is
known today, may be said to have reached
its peak when Sir Ralph Payne Gallwey
and Lord Walsingham
– 'two of the ten best shots in
England' – published their famous
book *Shooting in Field and Covert* in
the Badminton Library. By that time
clothes for shooting had changed. In
Britain, they haven't changed much
ever since. Nor has the code.**

THE WRONG SORT

With reservations the collector may reasonably assume that
'sporting' in England didn't become a gentleman's interest until
towards the end of the eighteenth century. It was then that
The Sportsmen's Directory (1792) recorded that 'the art of
shooting flying is arrived at tolerable perfection'.

By the standards of an earlier time, in an age when the
London gunmakers in a burst of invention and a patience
of exquisite craftsmanship were starting to lead the world, the
claim was fair enough. But it was still a relative one. Before,
when shooting was done with heavy single-barrelled weapons
with indifferent powder and barrels of forty-inches and more,
game brought to bag was stalked and shot sitting, often over a
bait. The gun was little more than an extension of the net and
the gin to collect food for the table. The coming of lighter guns,
better balanced with shorter barrels and smaller bores, per-
mitted a significant advance. It introduced the world of the
sporting aquatints.

Study the beautiful example of the English style, published
in 1807, which is the frontispiece of this book. Two shooters,
each with a brace of pointers, the one honouring the other's
nose, have flushed a covey of partridges. Properly, the pointers

19

BURBERRYS WEATHERPROOF KIT

PROOFED BY BURBERRYS in the yarn, in the thread and in the piece, is permanently antagonistic to rain and all forms of moisture.

ACTIVELY REPELS WET, being woven from fine and non-absorbent threads, retains its light-weight after exposure to downpours of rain.

LEVEL TEMPERATURE is maintained because the natural ventilating properties of Burberry are unaffected by the proofing.

BY GENIAL WARMTH, efficient powers of protection and absence of cumbrous weight, Burberry promotes a delightful feeling of comfort whatever the weather.

The Burberry.

The Burberry.

The ONE Top-coat Weatherproof in which good shooting can be maintained throughout a wet day.

Naturally ventilating, and yet proof against the assaults of rain, sleet and cold winds.

Light-in-weight and planned for liberty, it allows splendid freedom for rapid movement.

Burberry Suit.

Practical in design, smart in style and accurately balanced, with Pivot Sleeves and expanding pleats to give absolute freedom for limbs and muscles, and perfect the correspondence between sight and action.

ILLUSTRATED AND PATTERNED CATALOGUES
:: POST FREE. ::

BURBERRY SUIT.

30 to 33, Haymarket, LONDON; 10, Boul. Malesherbes, PARIS;
BASINGSTOKE; and Appointed Agents in Provincial Towns.

The figures in the Burberry's advertisement (1910) represent the sartorial mood at the turn of the century. Little changed except that shooting men were all using hammerless breechloaders rather than hammer guns. An exception was King George V, a fine game shot who used Purdey's with hammers up to his death. He considered that the ears of the hammers helped him sight the target. It is interesting that the figure (*left*) is ranging his left arm up the barrel in the style that King George V favoured. It is an unusual gunhandling position, although essentially sound. Collectors of game-guns should note that barrel length is an indication of period. Thirty-inches was popular at the turn of the century. Twenty-eight and twenty-five inches is characteristic today.

ought to have dropped on charge; but the printmakers never stood on unbecoming detail. Nevertheless, they belonged to the period and, before the invention of photography, they tell us as much as we will ever comprehend.

I shall never know how they kept their hats on in covert. I stand to be corrected, but I have never discovered that any of them tackled an oncoming bird. All the sporting prints support that they shot going away birds for business, with an occasional crossing and behind bird for show. For preference, they took flat shots in which the gunner could hold his aim until the flint whizzed the charge after a hang on pressing the trigger of about a 10th of a second. It is significant that most of the early books put a greater emphasis on dog work than gun practice. A good pointer got a man more surely on his mark than a gun could.

The early sportsmen, who had arrived 'at tolerable perfection' in the art of shooting, were still at a disadvantage. In the interests of safety, as you will notice from the frontispiece and any other sporting print, they were advised to hold back their left hand so that it was just in front of the trigger guard. It was a precaution against the barrels bursting under fire. But, as a result, the gun was top heavy for the average shot. Captain Lacy, whose book *The Modern Shooter* (1842) I much admire, deplored the habit and recommended the modern method of balancing the gun evenly in both hands.

In his wisdom, Captain Lacy also emphasized the importance of settling the legs evenly and, according to height, fairly close together. The printmakers – I wonder if any of them ever used a gun – invariably depict the shooter with one leg struck well forward. The balance of the shooters in the print on the frontispiece could scarcely be more untidy. My own view is that neither of them would have hit the partridge dropping out of the picture. But that, like so much else in the period, is speculation.

What is certain is that gameshooting at the beginning of the nineteenth century was largely experimental, both on the part of gunmakers and shooters. It was, at best, a messy business. The elegantly dressed characters in the sporting prints came home with blackened hands and faces, sooted and smelling like their guns with the oily residue of black powder. They went into the field with as many accessories for their weapons as if they were travelling a baby. The bare minimum was ramrod, powder flask, shot pouch or belt, spare flints, turnscrew for the cock and a pricker for the touchhole. After twenty rounds or so, their guns coked up like old tobacco pipes. Their hats, after a season in the field, smelt like exploded rockets.

The hazards of the sport were formidable. In the excitement of the chase, sportsmen fired their own ramrods after departing game. In the hurry to reload after a hangfire, which was common, there was always the danger that looking down the barrel to see what had gone wrong they would catch a charge in the face. If powder was poured into the barrel over a winking spark after shooting, flasks were liable to blow up.

Flint or percussion, the story wasn't much different. But the people of the time seem to have been astonishingly casual, probably ignorant of some of the risks they were taking. One reads of men who measured their powder out of the bowl of a broken clay pipe, collected a handful of mixed shot out of their pockets to top it.

The early writers tried to regulate shooting practice. After expounding their theories on the correct measurements of shot and powder for different bores, mostly founded on personal theory, they recognized a starting list of 'don'ts'. It is interesting that they regarded it as dangerous to carry a muzzleloader, as we carry breechloaders today, in the crook of the arm. They reckoned that the safer way was over the shoulder. But they also recommended heating black powder before shooting in plates 'too hot to hold'. It is proper to add that they cautioned it should be done away from open fires and candles. They gave instructions for loading, fair enough when men had to push powder and shot down the business end of a barrel, which make me wince. It was never safe: but they were a courageous lot.

I often think of them coming home after their days in field, covert and marsh, with their stinking guns and small prize of game, as if I had lived with them. No self-respecting housewife can have allowed the guns into the house. They had to be scrubbed out with cold water, and then hot water from a kettle, outside; the percussion arms, after the corrosion of the caps, even more thoroughly than the flintguns. When the guns were cleaned, the gunner himself equally needed a scour in the hip-bath.

The flintgun shooters of the sporting prints, largely because of the time it took to explode the charge, had to be pot-hunters; although improvements in the arms enabled them to take more sporting chances than their fathers. It is astonishing that, before the nineteenth century was little more than half over, their sons had passed through the detonator and the pinfire gun into the modern breechloader.

Shooting men didn't accept any of the new inventions without argument, even resentment. Many of them, including the redoubtable Colonel Peter Hawker, hung on to their old weapons long after they were outdated. The modern collector must relate weapons to the actual date they were widely used. In general, call it about twenty-five years after the first patent. Earlier types of guns were built long after new devices came in.

The Rev. Alexander Forsyth's patent for his detonating gun was registered in 1807; but it wasn't until 1820–30, after a flush of patents, that most of the conversions from flintlock to percussion were made. The coming of the percussion gun made it possible to shoot as efficiently, although not so quickly, as a breechloader today.

But it's doubtful if the art of shooting driven game was recognized much before 1840. By that time the breechloader had overtaken the muzzleloader. Yet the sporting breechloader introduced in 1850, didn't come into general use until the sixties.

It would be wrong to ascribe the time lag entirely to unreadiness in the sportsmen of the period to accept new inventions. No century in human history was hungrier for change than the nineteenth. The fact is that the first detonators weren't as good as the old flintguns, the early breechloaders weren't as good as the old detonators.

THE MUZZLELOADER TODAY

There are collectors of old arms with no desire to shoot them, just as there are people who collect other antiques with no wish to display them. I am not one of them. I belong with the outward looking individuals who enjoy action. It is important to tell how far an enthusiast with an old weapon can reasonably go.*

The safe way is to use replicas, which are increasingly manufactured. The Japanese are currently making a game of shooting with reproductions of matchlocks; the Americans practice with modern versions of the Kentucky rifle and various Colts. The play is not to my own taste. For me, the charm is to handle the stuff of history – to warm my palms on the burnished walnut of an old stock, to listen to the sweet double click of the action of a period cock or hammer, to put straight powder through the beautiful figuring of Damascus barrels. But it calls for care.

In all shooting there is an unavoidable element of risk. With old muzzleloaders, in which the metal of the barrel is almost certainly 'tired', the danger is greater. It could not be otherwise in a thing which has so far outlasted the human brain and muscle which created it. Handling muzzleloaders calls for very conscious discipline and attention to firing detail.

There is little doubt that the old sportsmen took risks. In many cases they suffered the consequences from burst barrels, powder flasks blowing up in their hands, and charges which went off in their faces. It is also true that others who spilt powder and shot into their guns, as liberally as some scoop mustard on to their dinner plates, got away with it. Black powder, as devilishly combustible outside a gun barrel as modern smokeless powders are relatively innocent until they are put inside one, can be exploded, as any firework addict knows, from a paper tube. The hazard in an old gun comes when a charge of lead is put on top of the powder. With the

* Enthusiasts are warmly recommended to contact that flourishing society "The Muzzleloaders Association".

24

increase it creates in pressure it is well to remember the admonition on the Roman Candle. After lighting the blue touch-paper, retire immediately.

In self-preservation, if you are firing a gun which has probably been silent for a hundred years, lash it to a fence or, better, a heavy tripod of the type used for sawing logs. You can test it with a light charge by pulling the trigger at the end of a long piece of string. Theoretically, the weapon should first be taken to a gunsmith to remove the breech-plugs and make an assessment of its condition. In practice he will not be able to give more than qualified approval. But you can proof it yourself by remote control, aiming the barrels at sheets of newspaper – which will show how the shot is patterning – and increasing the powder charge until you can reasonably take the risk of bringing the gun to your shoulder. When the gun is in your hands, however confident you feel, resist the temptation of loading a full charge. It is dangerous; and not even necessary. A muzzleloader of 14-bore, the equivalent of the modern 12-bore breechloader, will throw a killing pattern with 2 drachms of powder and an oz. of shot.

The correct balance of the charge will vary from gun to gun because muzzleloaders, whatever their nominal bores, are individuals. When you use one you must discover the mean charge of powder and shot which suits it; and suits you. Reading what the old gunners pontificated can be utterly confusing because shot sizes in their day were not uniform, and powder was variable in its efficiency. The contemporary shot with a light muzzleloader will do well to stick to No. 5 or No. 6 shot, and trust to light charges of powder, powder which is far more regular than anything they knew at the beginning of the nineteenth century.

Imperial Metal Industries (Kynoch) Ltd. sell four types of black powder today, graded by quality and grain size. TS2 and TS6 are best quality, types F and FFF are lower quality. TS2 or FFF should be used for 12-bore and smaller gauges, TS6 or F for 10-bore and larger.

A gun can be 'chambered' for the shot charge that suits

it by slipping an overcard into the mouth of the barrel. The load that settles evenly over the card is likely to be the best one for the gun. For overpowder wads in a 14-bore, I cut 12-bore felts, chewing them in my teeth so that they ram smoothly into the barrel. The old gunners favoured a bit of dry grass or tow to tamp the shot down. I prefer a bit of crumpled newspaper for the pyrotechnic effect it produces when the gun is fired.

Flintguns in shootable condition are necessarily rarer than percussion arms; but they still exist. The trouble is to obtain reliable flints. Gun flints are still knapped at Brandon in Suffolk, but most of them are now so soft that the gunner is unlikely to get more than four or five shots from them. But I have flints now, 'the transparent black flints' recommended by Colonel Peter Hawker, specially knapped for one of my own guns, which are good for twenty shots. The art of getting good performance is to mount the flint, with a piece of leather behind it, flat side upwards in the jaws of the cock so that it strikes evenly on the frizzen. After wear, it can be turned over. Suffice that there is a craft in settling a flint efficiently which provides a satisfaction all of its own.

By comparison, mounting copper caps on the nipples of a percussion gun has no problems. The snag, with both forms of ignition, is that they don't work unless touchholes and nipples are kept scrupulously free from blockage. No accessory is more useful to the modern muzzleloading enthusiast than a woman's hairpin to push powder and fulminate waste out of the way. And there is no duty more rewarding in result than thorough gun-cleaning.

A flintgun can be orphaned from care, reddened with the rust from powder residue, without coming to much harm. A percussion gun, poisoned with the chemicals from the cap, can go to pot very quickly without constant attention. But neither sort of gun will give a good performance in the field without thorough nannying. Oiling and polishing, useful enough, are far less important than the scouring and pumping out of the barrels with libations of cold water, followed by hot to steam them dry.

From the end of the eighteenth century to the twentieth, this figure typifies the pattern of the man who emerged with the evolution of sporting guns. John Buckle, head gamekeeper of Merton, Norfolk, in the eighties, was the grandson of 'Old' Watson who died in 1834, the son of Israel Buckle, who died in 1873. Between them they spanned the development of the game gun from the flintlock to the breechloader, from pot-shooting to the days of huge bags, and guns who expended twenty thousand rounds a season. John Buckle is wearing velveteens, moleskin waistcoat, buttoned leggings and the hard hat which was the uniform of a keeper of the time. He carries a long-barrelled hammer gun, with Damascus barrels.

Modern cleaning equipment, although it should be kept apart from the jags and brushes used for breechloaders, is ideal for the job. The important thing, as you pump the rod, is to force the black and oily residue through the touch-holes and the nipples until the water spouts clean.

The loading principle for both flint and percussion is the same. The best way is not the way recommended in Greener's book (page 13). The heel of the weapon should be firmly seated against the left boot. The barrels in the left hand should be pushed at the full length of the left arm into the stand-at-ease position. The object of the exercise is to keep your head out of the way if the gun goes off unexpectedly.

NORFOLK LIARS; At the end of the nineteenth century, when guns added up their individual bags, these were fashionable. The example (*left*) is a simple counter. The other (*right*) is rarer, a silver piece made by Thornhill, of 144 New Bond Street, with markers to score pheasants and hares; and, on the reverse, partridges and rabbits.

If it is a double barrelled gun, drop the ramrod into the empty barrel before you pour powder into the other. This is to prevent the notorious error of double-charging. Ram the powder down hard with the wad; and, when you have measured the shot, wad it down lightly – just enough to keep it in position in the barrel.

Remember all the risks: Double loading doubles the danger. A spark in the chamber from a previous shot can explode the powder as you pour it in. Make sure that your gun is never at full cock, especially when loading; and generally until you mean to fire. If you suspect you have made a mistake draw the charge with the wormscrew which is normally fitted under the brass nose of the ramrod.

It is useful to add that, among the risks for the guns themselves, you will almost certainly shatter the hammers of a detonator if you release the action on the nipples of an empty arm. You can spark an empty flintlock because the frizzen affords the necessary resistance. When any old gun comes into your hands, begin by searching it with the ramrod to make sure that some slaphappy sportsman in the past hasn't left a charge in it. It can happen; it has happened to me.

It may be that the reader will conclude that I have over-estimated the hazards of shooting with these old guns. It is the safe way to introduce them. But I wouldn't be writing this at all if I wasn't the victim of their seductive charms. I am one who makes no apology for a love affair with history.

Those who are enmeshed in it move into a period where language was made which lives beyond the language of its sport. Who hasn't 'ducked the flash' as the wildfowl used to when the old muzzleloaders fizzed laboriously into action? Who hasn't enjoyed a 'dram', slang which dates from a time when a drachm wasn't a measure of whisky but a measure of powder? Whose projects haven't 'hung fire' the way the muzzleloaders did?

EARLY BREECHLOADERS AND RIFLES

I have never fired an early breechloader. The weapons were fragile and evolutionary; and, although they represent an important phase in arms' history, they belong to the collector's cabinet rather than the open air. I have also a dread of late nineteenth century arms, proofed only for black powder, which turn up in the crook of the arm of people (often gamekeepers) using them with modern smokeless ammunition.

It is to the lasting credit of the old craftsmen that their weapons have stood up so long to the immoderate strain. How often I have had to tell a man, boasting of the hard-hitting qualities of his old gun (they always do) that, without the letters NP on the flats of the barrels, he is taking his life in his hands every time he shoots it.

My personal preference is for the muzzleloader; or the best contemporary breechloader. In this crowded island I am also reluctant to recommend the use of rifles, not excluding muzzle-loaders which, in the hands of an expert shot, are as deadly as the rifles of our own time. Even a muzzleloading pea rifle, the equivalent of a long rifled ·22, is effectively lethal up to a hundred yards at small targets.

In my library, I have a rare privately printed book of Sporting Sketches by a remarkable woman who wrote under the pseudonym of 'Diane Chasseresse'. She describes how in crinolines in the early fifties she shot running stag in the Highlands with a muzzleloading rifle she called 'Little Death'. Her name was Caroline Creyk. She died at the age of 101 years and nine months in 1946. It is a fragment of sporting history that, throughout the 1914–18 War, she kept 'Little Death' in an upstairs window of her house in Park Lane swearing that, if the Germans got to London, she would pick off the Kaiser at 400-yards.

This book is no attempt to represent a definitive picture. It simply offers a glimpse of English sporting arms in the nineteenth century to tempt the new collector to probe deeper. Latterly I have emphasized gun accessories and cartridges because these seem destined to become collectors' specialities in their own right.

AWAKENING THE DEAD

In these pages I have only shaken the shoulder of the past, offered a wink from the twilight world of the guns and gunners of the nineteenth century. My purpose is simply to brief the new collector in preparation for an excursion into the larger literature of a subject which, without the sort of guideline I have given, can fog the picture like black powder over a battlefield. Most of the old sporting writers are alarmingly prolix; and, until you know your way around them, even misleading.

In the beginning there was Colonel Peter Hawker whose work *Instructions to Young Sportsmen in all that relates to Guns and Shooting* (Ten editions, 1814–1854) is generally regarded as the Bible of Gameshooting. At the risk of excommunication from the company of St. Hubert, I think that it is not a good book. Important though it is for a student of the period,

Not the least of the charms of old arms are gunmakers' labels,
beautifully lettered and illustrated with swashes to match.
The date of these London makers is early nineteenth
century. The value of any old piece is immeasurably enhanced
if it is boxed in its original baize-lined case, with
its maker's label and a full complement of accessories. If
the receipted bill for the arm is there as well so much the better.

it is ill-constructed, peevish, snobbish and, in practical information, poorly presented. Hawker, the Hampshireman who fought under Wellington in the Peninsular, is revealed more rewardingly in his diaries (I recommend the version edited by Eric Parker).

In practical terms I much prefer Hawker's contemporary, Captain Lacy, whose work *The Modern Shooter* (1842) shows a remarkable prescience of modern shooting practice. Lacy, educated at Repton, was a Cheshireman with his feet square on the grass. His literary style is tiresome; but you can learn more from him about period shooting business than Hawker.

The student cannot ignore three encyclopedias of Rural Sports: *Rev. W. B. Daniel's* (*c.* 1753–1835), *Blaine* (1840), and *Stonehenge* (1855). In all but Daniel's, where there is some nice wooden type, the presentation is terrible. But there is enough inside to be worth a hunt providing you don't believe all they tell you.

Of the old books, I recommend you for entertainment to *Oakleigh's Shooting Code* and *Wilson and Oakleigh's Rod and*

Gun. Pierce Egan's Book of Sports gives a glimpse of the mood of the early part of the century. In the latter part, the most memorable works on shooting are W. W. Greener's book *The Gun and Its Development* (1881–1910); and the Badminton Library's *Shooting in Field and Covert* (1889) by Lord Walsingham and H. Payne Gallwey.

For a contemporary assessment of the past the best work is unquestionably J. N. George's *English Guns and Rifles*. George, unhappily, was killed in the war. What he has to say is as authoritative as you can get.

Of contemporary writers I recommend the chapter in Richard Arnold's book, *The Shooter's Handbook*, on muzzle-loading arms. For those who want to shoot the old weapons today, Arnold has the experience and the wisdom to advise. I would like you to read Thurlow Craig – the greatest wizard with a revolver I have ever met – in *Shooter's Delight*. He writes like a bird about the discovery of an old peagun rifle. If you are interested in *Air Guns and Air Rifles*, Leslie Wesley has written the definitive work. And, if you hope to become a connoisseur, you can reach for the heights by reading the brilliant piece of gun research on *The Mantons, Gunmakers* by W. Keith Neal and D. H. L. Back.

ESG–C

ENGLISH SPORTING GUNS
and accessories

BOOKS on antique arms are normally decorated with the choicest weapons and accessories the author can lay hands on. There are some beautifully preserved weapons here. But the new collector is unlikely – he could even be unwise – to start at the top.

So I make no excuse for introducing this gathering of arms with one, messed about by who-knows-who, and me, which represents the sort of material with which a new collector is likely to begin. Overleaf is a single-barrelled flintgun by Henry Nock incorporating his patent breech (to which I have referred earlier) and made in the last years of the eighteenth century. It isn't much more valuable now than a riveted piece of bone china. But brokendown weapons offer the best introduction to the fascinating period they belonged to.

I commend you to begin collecting with 'any old iron'. Whatever their condition, all antique arms are rewarding. They were fashioned at a time when the workmen were equipped with little more than a file, and lamp black to confirm the finishing of a movement. It is something of a miracle, in a machine age, that craftsmen's hands achieved what they did. You can pick up old guns, whose outward parts are in ruins, and find that the action – the mainspring under pressure for a hundred and fifty years – sings when you release it. A handmade breech-loading gun, in good condition, won't close satisfactorily against a thin piece of paper on the face of the breech block.

All arms collectors, even those with clumsy hands, should be encouraged, like medical students with dead bodies, to examine how they are put together. In practice it is not even very difficult. While I cannot recommend an amateur, unless he happens to be a master with a turnscrew, to remove the locks from a modern breechloader, it is easy to open a muzzleloading one. A single screw, or two sidenails, contains the actions. All that is necessary to remember is to half cock the gun to release the triggers to let the actions out or in.

The man with a modest purse is already unlikely to win in the high game. But as I write in 1969 it is still possible to collect at reasonable prices. The best opportunity for new collectors

lies more probably in the acquisition of cartridges and gun accessories.

I remember that as a boy I used to follow the shooting men in the field, sniffing the fragrant smell of the expended cartridges, collecting the paper cases in my pockets. I little thought then that they could become collectors' items; but they have. In the evolutionary succession from brass, half-brass and paper, through aluminium to plastic, the jackdaws in the collecting world have a new game. The names and the colours of the great gunmakers of the day offer a challenge almost as rich as stamp-collecting.

It is also sure that the accessories of the sporting gun, ignored by collectors until comparatively recently, will make their place as 'jewellery' of a man's world. The invention of the nineteenth century gunmakers, remarkable as it was in arms, was as pretty as a boutique in its nonsense.

The lesson, it applies to all old things, is that if you keep them long enough posterity will give them the recognition of what may be called romantic disuse. The powder flasks and the shot pouches I have shown on these pages might well have been thrown away, as most of them were, when their time was done. Some survived in attics; so some are here to remind us of an earlier generation. The luck in history is always what somebody was too lazy to destroy. The charm of it is the recollection that the people who belonged – in this context, those pot hatted characters with their muzzleloaders – were just like us, the sort of chaps it would have been fun to swop pints of beer with.

With an old gun in your hands, with the imagination to recreate the people who used it, you are in effect extending a lifetime far beyond your own.

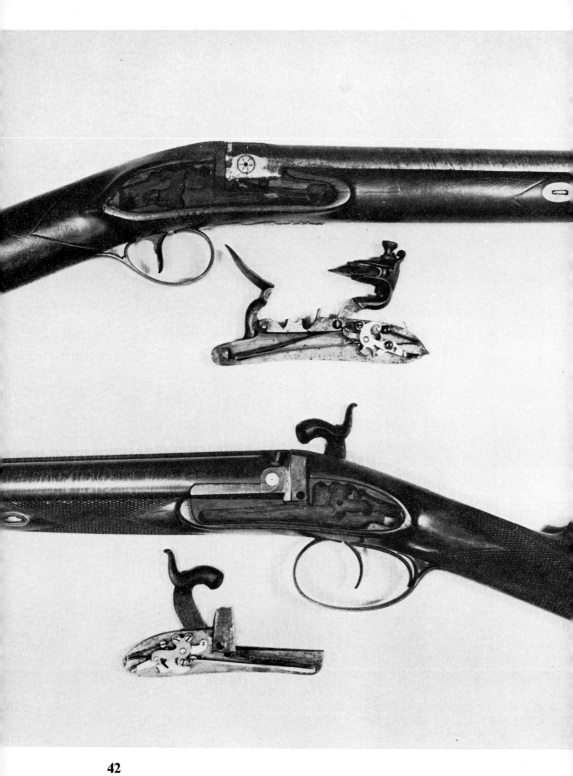

There is no better way to get to know old arms, to assess their quality, than to study the workmanship of the locks, the complex hand-carving of the wood which seats them. In generations to come guns of the nineteenth century – and the present one too – will be admired among the most wondrous things that man's hand has contrived. They will, to my mind, become the old masters of tomorrow. At present sporting guns of the English kind – it is proper to add Scottish and Irish, too, both countries which produced superlative weapons – are commanding at auction prices rising at every sale. Their value will undoubtedly continue to increase as mechanization replaces the vintage products of the hand craftsmen. The collector who treasures them has a responsibility beyond his personal interest, however battered the piece, however shaky it has become with age.

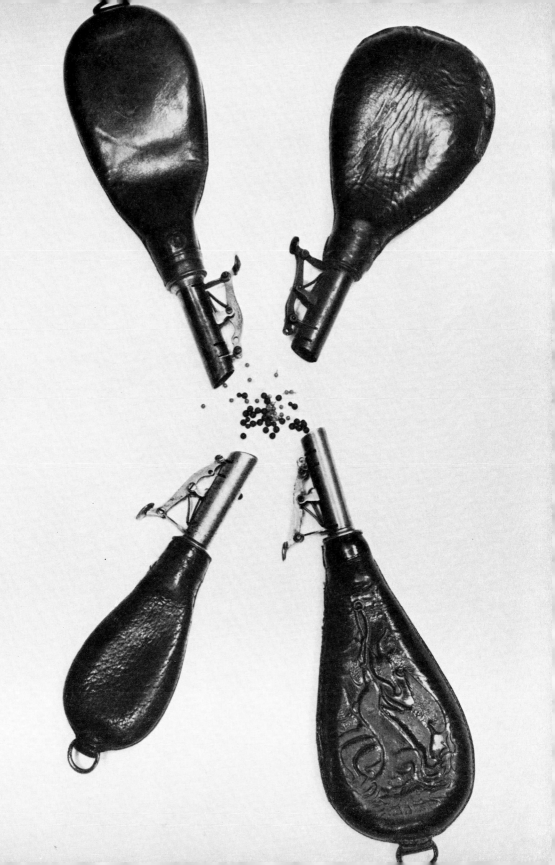

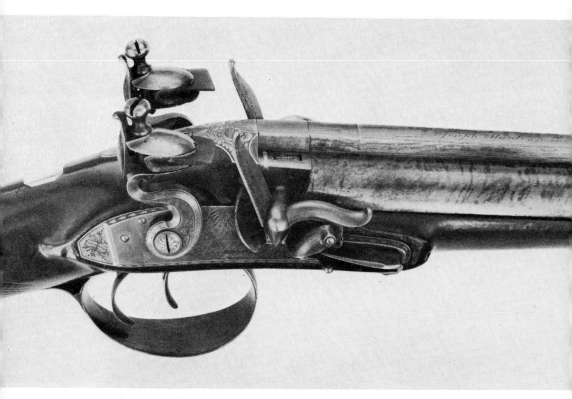

JOSEPH MANTON'S ELEVATING RIB
Patent No. 2966, September 1806
(Incorporated in D B Flintlock made in 1807)
Colonel Peter Hawker composed this epitaph carved on Manton's
tombstone in the cemetery at Kensal Green; 'In memory of
Mr. Joseph Manton who died, universally regretted, on the 29th
day of June, 1835, aged 69. This humble tablet is placed by his
afflicted family, mainly to mark where are deposited his mortal
remains. But an everlasting monument to his unrivalled genius
is already established in every quarter of the globe, by his
celebrity as the greatest artist in firearms that ever this
world produced, as the founder and the father of the modern gun
trade and as a most scientific inventor in other departments,
not only for the benefit of his friends and the sporting
world, but for the good of King and Country.'

46

JOSEPH MANTON'S PERCUSSION TUBE LOCK
Patent No. 4285, August 1818
(Manton's refinement of the Forsyth patent of 1807)
Not all 'Joe's' contemporaries were as uncritical in their
eulogies as Hawker. Many preferred the work of his less
spectacular brother, John. Captain Lacy (edited here for brevity)
said: 'As a practical workman he was below mediocrity; but
as a great general in the head, if not the hands, he was
unrivalled. No man was a better judge of gunwork, or had a finer
taste. And if, occasionally, he might get credit for an invention
which was not altogether his own, he rarely recommended any
novelty to the public of which either party had cause to repent.'
But the *mot juste* on him is probably that attributed to
another gunmaker; 'But for him we should all of us have
been a parcel of blacksmiths.'

FORSYTH'S DETONATING LOCK
Patent No. 3032, April 1807
Still a muzzleloader, Forsyth's gun, with
his Patent Roller Primers, was the invention which
effectively marked the beginning of the end of the
age of flint. Forsyth guns enjoyed a considerable
popularity in their own right until they were
superseded in due course by simplified forms of
percussion. The Rev. Forsyth, the Scottish clergyman,
looms large in nineteenth century gun development.

48

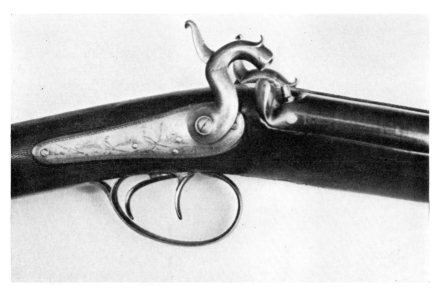

Contrast the slender shape of this 12-bore percussion
arm by Ancell of Perth (1830–40) with the Forsyth
gun (*opposite*) which showed the way. Its lockplates
decorated with engravings of green plover and cock
pheasants, its hammers curved like cobras ready to
strike, here is the technical achievement of a mere quarter century.

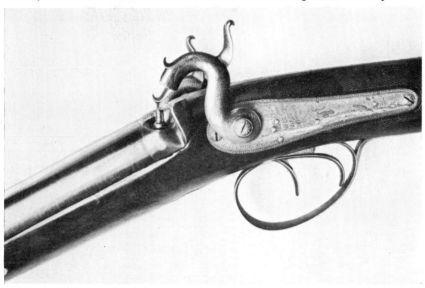

In a period of swift change, Charles Jones' patent of 1833 is one of the hybrids, a muzzleloading percussion gun reaching for the advantage of an enclosed detonating system. Described as a central fire muzzleloading double gun it had a transitional popularity. Jones (1825–35) was gunmaker to Prince Albert.

The external hammers, for cocking purposes only, are blind. The special feature is the thumb slide to waterproof the locks. The caps were placed on the nose of the hammers, and had the detonating composition outside on the crown of the cap. Evidence of the variations of gun design through a generation.

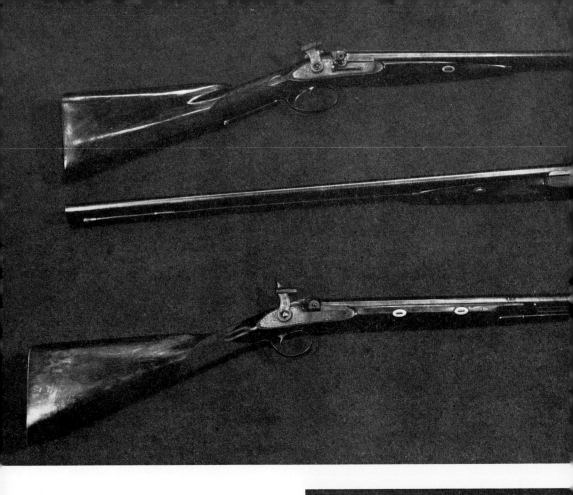

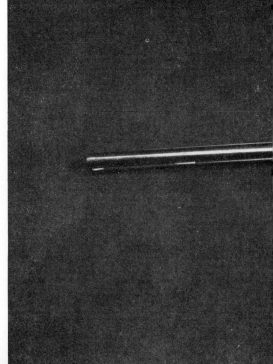

In its last golden years the English sporting flintgun achieved a beauty of form and balance as aesthetic as the orders of classical architecture. From then until now the 'building' of guns, irrespective of refinements in the actions, remains virtually unchanged.

52

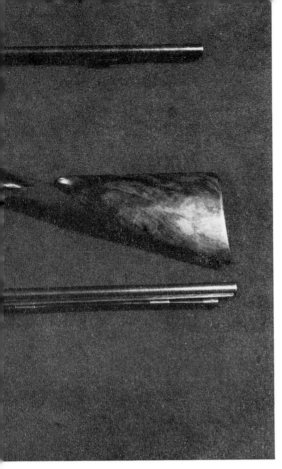

A Joseph Manton tube lock. . . .
A John Manton double percussion
gun. . . . A Joseph Manton
conversion from flint to percussion. . . .
Decade by decade throughout the
first half of the nineteenth
century new inventions tumbled
over each other in a bewildering
complexity of small detail. But
these semi-silhouettes outline
one factor which was constant.

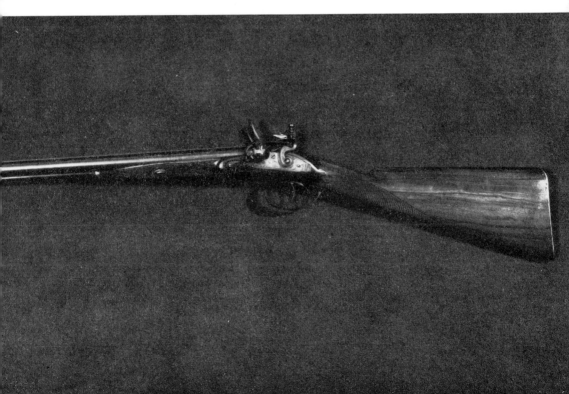

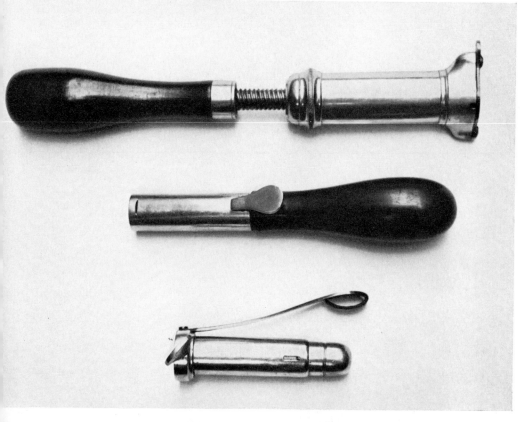

The unfamiliar hand tools
of a pinfire reloader. *Top*,
is the cylindrical turnover,
middle is a paper
case lengths cutter (not
necessarily pinfire), and
below is a recapper for
pushing a new pin into the
base of the cartridge.

The way out for the powder
flasks and shot pouches. With
the coming, and albeit quick
departure, of pin and needlefire
guns, old friends got
lost in the attic. See pages
44 and 45.

54

Of the intermediate arms, before the breechloader was successfully married to the centre-fire cartridge, the reign of the pin fire was the briefest. But, with the invention of the gastight cartridge with a metallic base, it enjoyed a world wide popularity and remained in use long after the hammerless ejector gun had rendered it obsolete. This is a double-barrelled 12-bore, with an underlever closing, by John Blissett.

The French gunmaker LeFaucheux is attributed with the invention
of the first successful breechloader. Adopting the pinfire
cartridge, he first marketed it on the Continent in the eighteen
forties. It attracted no attention from the English gun
trade until it was shown at the Great Exhibition of 1851. It was
introduced in England, shortly after, by Joseph Lang.

In 1852, Charles Lancaster invented this centre-fire
gun with extractors. Designed to shoot the original base fire
cartridge, the barrels move forward a short distance
before dropping. An extended hook slides under the standing
breech and the underlever closes the gun. Little was
left to invent now except the true hammerless self-ejector.

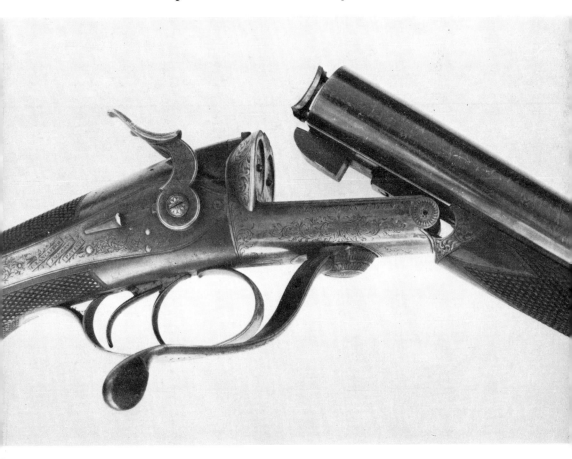

JOSEPH NEEDHAM'S NEEDLEGUN
Patent No. 184, October 1852
Needham's invention, with barrels fixed to the stock
like a muzzleloader, was designed for chamber-loading
with a central fire cartridge. The gun is cocked
by swinging the finger tab towards the top of the barrel,
and pulling the engraved chamber cover outward to insert
the cartridge. When the double-block is returned to
its place the gun is ready for firing.

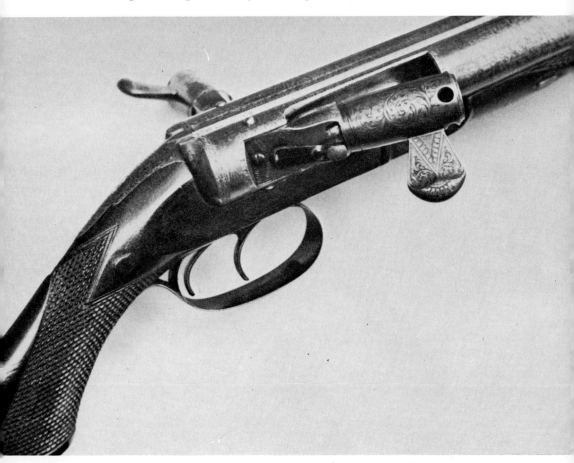

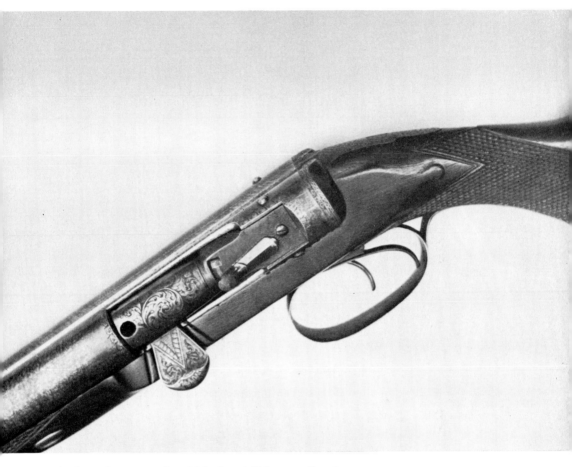

An ingenious arm, in which the striking needle pierces
through the outer envelope of the cartridge, for a time
it had considerable success. It was doomed, as so many
other patents of the period, by the quick advance of
simpler and better systems. For the creative gunmaker it
was a frustrating period in which new devices tumbled
over each other in a bewildering succession of new improvements.

In 1870 – the date is arguable – Purdey introduced
this double-barrelled 12-bore pinfire gun. Its importance
is that this seems to be the earliest model showing the
top lever and sliding bolt action which is basically
the Purdey gun today. Collectors should be very
careful in assigning definitive years to improvements. The
Purdey action is incorporated in a later patent (No. 397
of January 1878) and described again in Beesley's patent of 1880.

In 1874, Lancaster made his 12-bore gun fitted with Needham's
Patent Cartridge Ejector. At the start it was ineffective.
By the end of the century, self-ejector guns were efficient.
Today they are faultless. But it is well to remember that
precisely when all the gremlins were eliminated is part of
what used to be called 'the mystery of gunmaking'. The
name of a maker on the gunbarrel often conceals the
invention of an anonymous workman.

61

Theophilus Murcott patented his hammerless doublegun
in 1871 with sidelocks and a push down underlever.
From its then strange boxlike appearance, and the loud
noise it made in closing, it was nicknamed 'Murcott's
Mousetrap'. English attempts to introduce hammerless
guns had been made, but without success. Murcott's was
a decided advance as it has a safety lever moving in an
arc on the top of the action prominently in view and
easy to get at. Although the gun only enjoyed moderate
success – it was heavy and noisy – it marked a turning
point. Henceforward the hammerless gun had come to stay.

In the eighteen twenties, thirties, forties, fifties – how
difficult it is to get the date right – it was reverse
arms for the muzzleloader. This Deighton gun – a pride of
the flintlock period – was dismissed within a generation as obsolete
as a chimney pot hat. Look at it, and wonder at the craftsmanship.

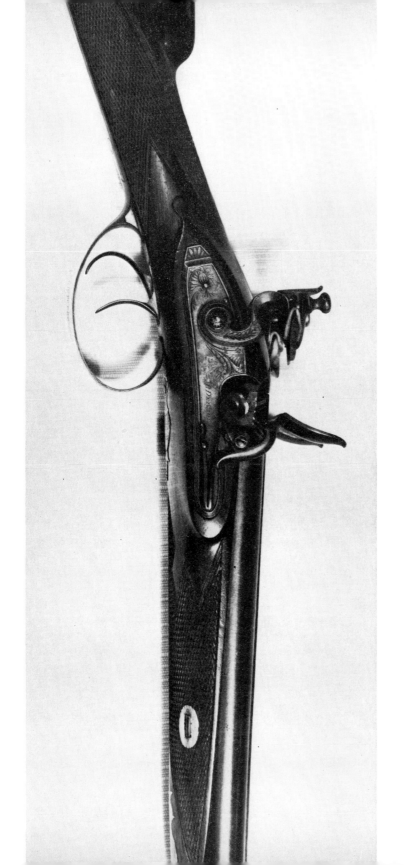

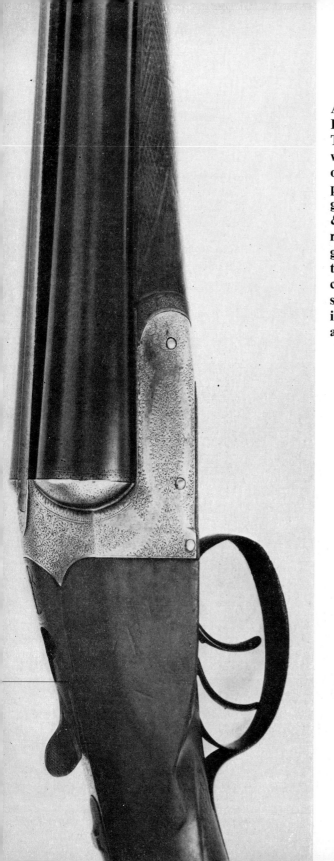

ANSON & DEELEY BOXLOCK
Patent No. 1756, May 1875
The gunmaker W. W. Greener (1910), with the built-in disinclination of his trade to give unnecessary praise to others' inventiveness, generously described the Anson & Deeley Patent as 'the first really successful hammerless gun'. In early models, of the type illustrated here, the closure was not entirely satisfactory. But, with subsequent improvements, it is the stoutest action ever devised.

An A & D boxlock, as it came to be called, gave quicker ignition and, with a strong mainspring and a short hammer blow, introduced a mechanism which is still the most widely used gun action today. Sidelocks have better breeding. Boxlocks, with their simplicity of action—albeit lacking the long limbed shape of the traditional beauties of the London craft—are working guns without parallel

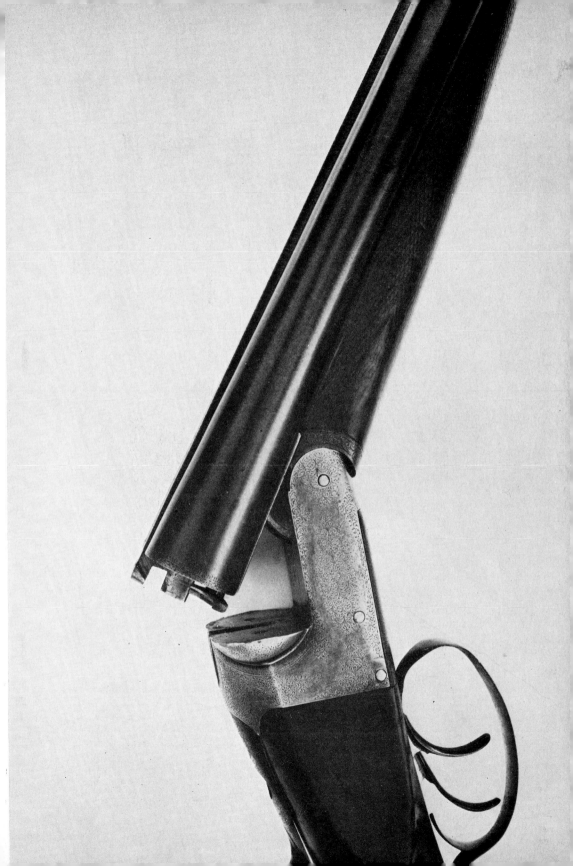

Tubes to convert one bore of gun to another are available today. Our forefathers struggled with conversion chambers from one form of ignition to another. *Left,* to make a pinfire gun take a ribbed percussion cap. *Middle,* centre fire converter to percussion. *Right,* 'everlasting' pinfire cartridge case.

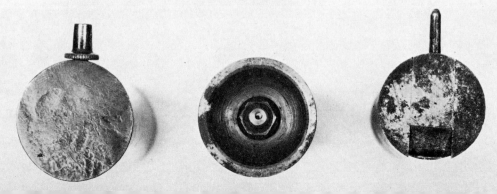

DEVELOPMENT OF CARTRIDGES (from left to right)
Kynoch 4-bore full brass case; Eley 12-bore
3 in. loaded with Eley Patent Wire Shot Cartridge;
Kynoch .410 full brass case; Eley 32-bore gastight;
Eley full brass case; E. H. Daw's Patent, the first
true central fire cartridge in Britain; Eley patent
wire shot cartridge; 15-bore for 14-bore
muzzle-loader; 12 mm pinfire; 14-bore pinfire;
Eley 10-bore pinfire, early brass case.

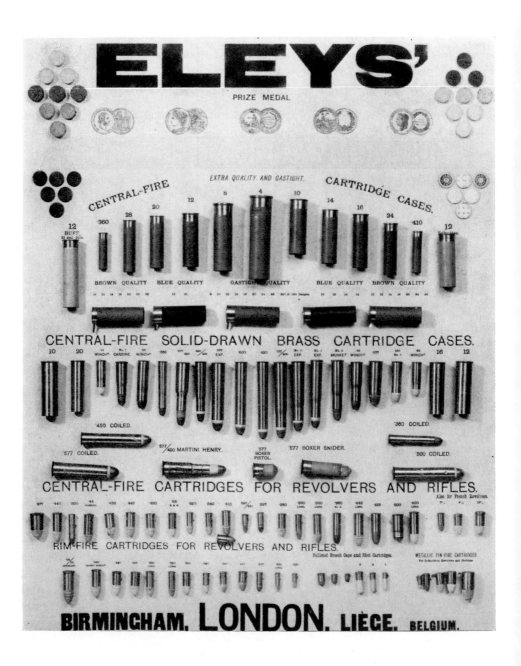

Wielding shoulder guns of up to 22 pounds, the nine-teenth century fowlers used cartridges like these. The Eley 2-bore case and the Kynoch 4-bore are ranged to scale beside a modern 12-bore crimped cartridge. The gunmen did not necessarily charge their huge cases to the limit. A length cutter was used to trim them to taste.

There is no question that cartridges, still resting in old pigskin bags today, will be the collectors' items of tomorrow. Increasingly, the traditional English gunmakers now look to Imperial Metal Industries, still incorporating the old names of Kynoch and Eley, for a standard product with only minor variations in loads. The new cartridge (*bottom right*) is waterproof, non-corrosive, and consistent to a degree that no hand-loaded cartridge could ever be. Good reason why collectors will increasingly treasure these paper cases, in all the colours of the spectrum, loaded in the past by the great makers themselves. In the top two rows are a few of them; in the bottom row, a glimpse of contemporary products.

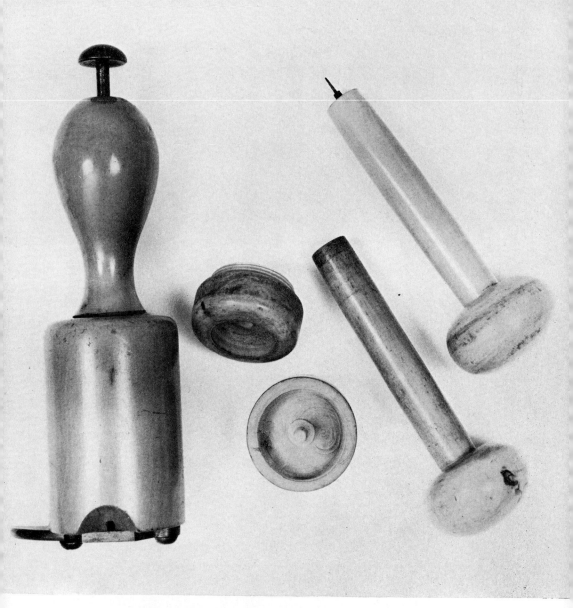

Handloading was practised more extensively in the
past than it is now. While the memory of the muzzleloaders
was still green, sportsmen liked to experiment
with charges best suited to their individual weapons
and themselves. This beautiful boxwood reloading kit is
adapted for both pinfire and centre fire cartridges.

The tools of handloading
have changed very little
in half a century, and
more. The capper and recapper
(*bottom right*) primes the empty
cartridge case. The funnel
(*bottom left*) is for
charging the cartridge. It
also incorporates a turnover
for closing the rim.
The device (*above*) is
a simple turnover.

An 'Erskine' cartridge
reloading box, adapted for
both centre and pinfire
cases. The diagonal slits
in the wood house the pin
in the latter. The box
houses twenty-six
12-bore cases which are
locked into position by
the slide. The box is
then turned over; and
powder, wad shot and
overcard rammed into the
cases. It is ranged for
a black powder load from
$2\frac{1}{2}$ to $3\frac{1}{4}$ drachms, and a
shot charge from 1 to $1\frac{1}{4}$
ozs. An increment slide
(*below right*) can be
hinged over the charging
frame to increase the
load by $\frac{1}{2}$ drachm of powder
and $\frac{1}{4}$oz of shot.

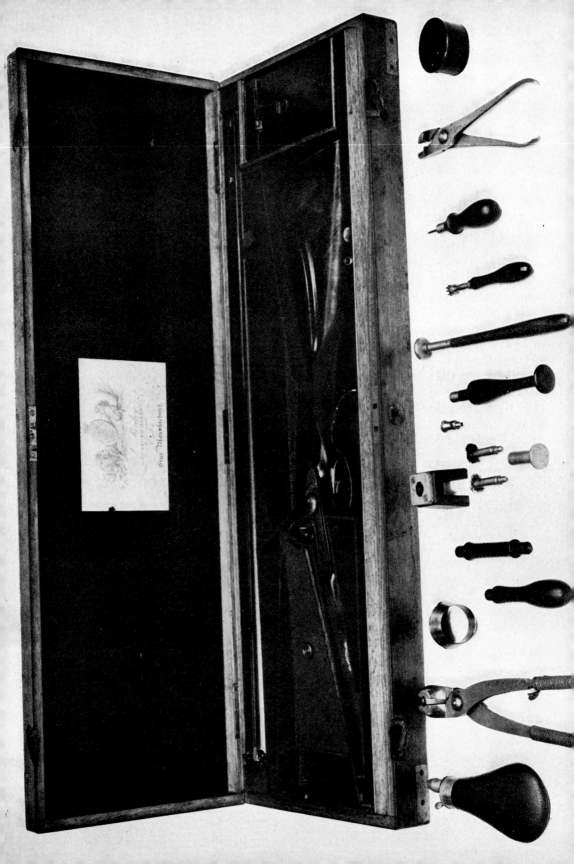

he flamboyance of the nineteenth century is reflected
ere, its taste for guncases furnished cost regardless. The
nmakers weren't slow to provide a range of gadgets for
e most improbable contingencies. The rifle (*opposite*),
ith its trousseau, was built by Purdey for the famous
ot, Lord Huntingfield.

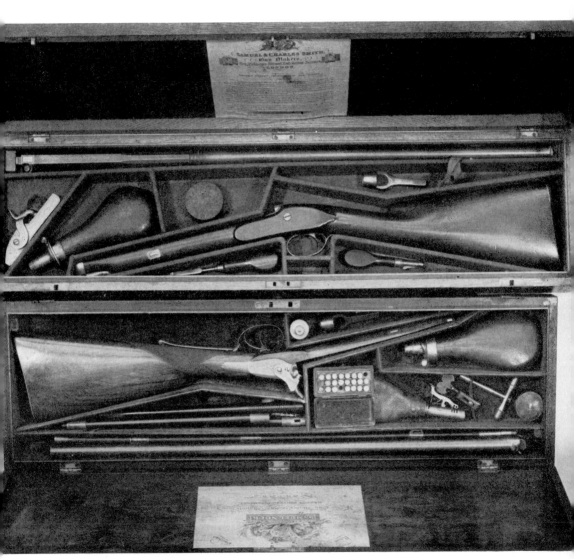

The single-barrelled 14-bore percussion gun (*above*) is
overwhelmed by its own wardrobe of accessories, almost all
of them 'patents' of one sort or another. The double-
barrelled 15-bore patchlock gun by Samuel Nock (*below*)
incorporates 'Nock's patent grip safety and twenty
spare strikers primed with patchcaps'.

77

Among the multiple accessories in old gun cases, the one
most likely to be missing is the turnscrew. The reason
is that turnscrews were usually worked out of the fine
tempered steel of old mainsprings. Many were adopted
for other purposes. What got left presents a problem for
the collector as puzzling as the initiation of a torturer's
apprentice. On the following pages, regardless of order, is
a test of identification. The brief answers are on page 85.

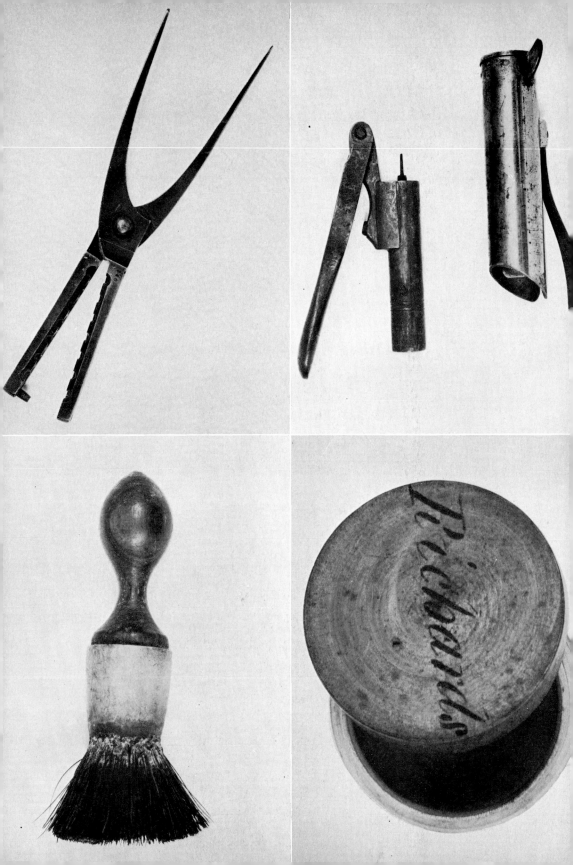

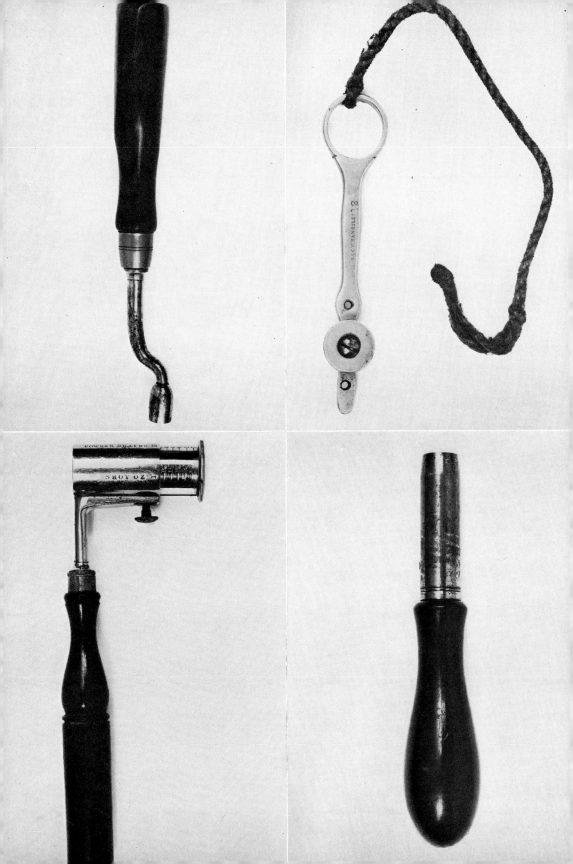

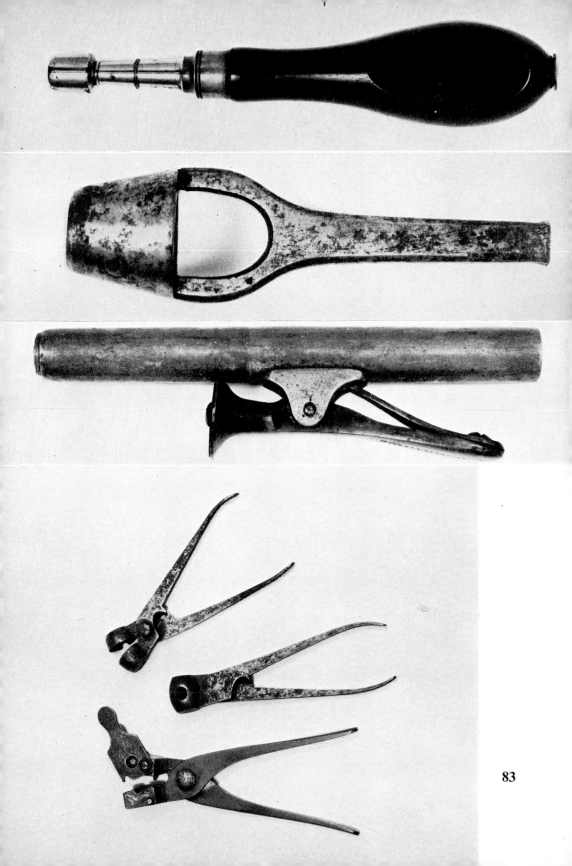

79 *Top left,* brass percussion cap dispenser. *Top right,* paper case ironer. *Bottom left,* combined percussion nipple key, oil bottle with pricker cap, and spare nipples in handle. *Bottom right,* six-star hand crimper for 10-bore brass cartridge.

80 *Top left,* mould for casting swan drops. *Top right,* .410 de and recapping tool, and paper cartridge length cutter. *Bottom left,* brush for cleaning nipples and touch holes. *Bottom right,* wood box for spare set of hammergun strikers.

81 *Top left,* adjustable powder and shot measure. *Top right,* double powder and shot measure. *Bottom left,* pneumatic nipple primer. Needle cleans vent and reprimes. *Bottom right,* Britannia metal oil bottle.

82 *Top left,* striker key for hammer gun. *Top right,* centre fire and pinfire cartridge extractor. *Bottom left,* measure for powder and shot. *Bottom right,* cartridge rammer.

83 *Top,* nipple key with pricker in handle, 20-bore wad cutter, paper cartridge length cutter. *Below,* pincer type bullet moulds with spare cutters.

84 *Top,* hammernose cleaning tool, nipple cleaning tool, 12-bore pinfiring loading funnel. *Below,* 10-bore Kynoch brass case hand crimper

85 *Top,* 8-bore Kynoch full length brass cased crimper. *Below,* shot charger for double gun.

85

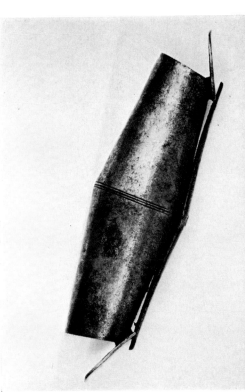

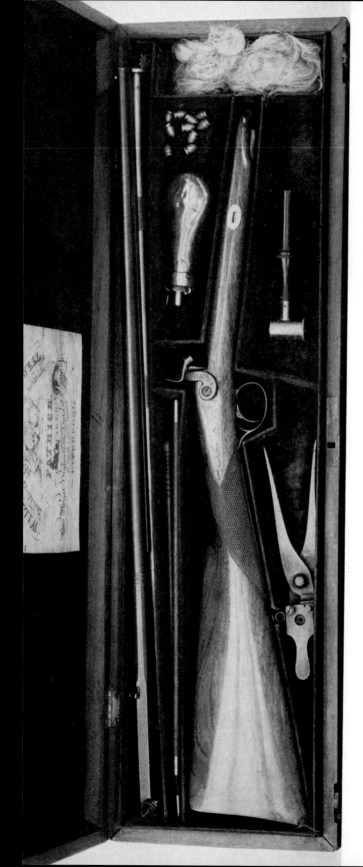

A single-barrelled .34 percussion sporting rifle made by Williams & Powell, of Liverpool. It is a small bored arm, useful for shooting small game, of a type popularly known as a pea rifle. By comparison with the rifles on pages 76–77 it will be noted that this one is cased with only bare necessities.

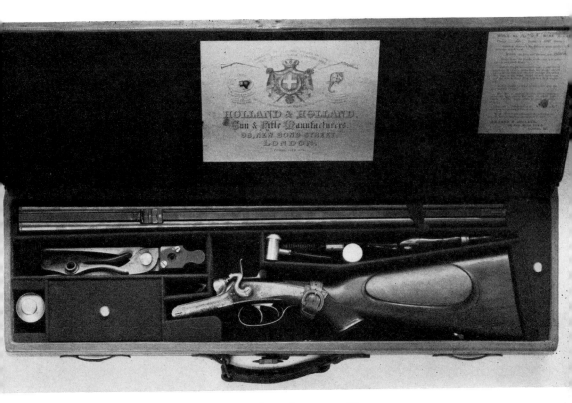

A double-barrelled .450 Express top-lever hammer rifle
by Holland & Holland. The smallbore rifle (*opposite*) was
almost certainly designed for shooting in England. The
Holland & Holland gun is of a calibre popular at the time
in India; although it could have been used for stalking
in the Highlands of Scotland.

A 7-barrelled volley rifle by Henry Nock. Originally
a short range naval carbine, these flint guns
firing all barrels with one pressure of the trigger, became
popular with goose-shooters. The pattern was erratic,
the penetration effective!

A 4-barrelled hammerless gun – with 'patent oval smooth
bore rifling, and internal rotating striker' – made by
Charles Lancaster. It fired only one round at a time
It was inevitably displaced by magazine loading.

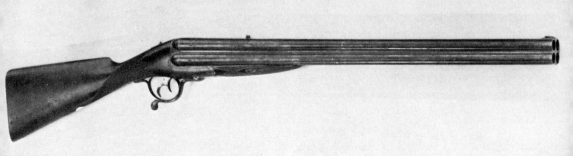

A double-barrelled 30-bore percussion sporting rifle by
Wilkinson & Son with 24-inch barrel. It was probably
intended for deer-shooting. Percussion rifles when
meticulously loaded shot up to contemporary accuracy

A breechloader with a 31 inch .577 rifled barrel made
by Prince & Green. The specimens on these two pages
illustrate the variations in the bore size, barrel length
and actions before rifles were relatively standardized.

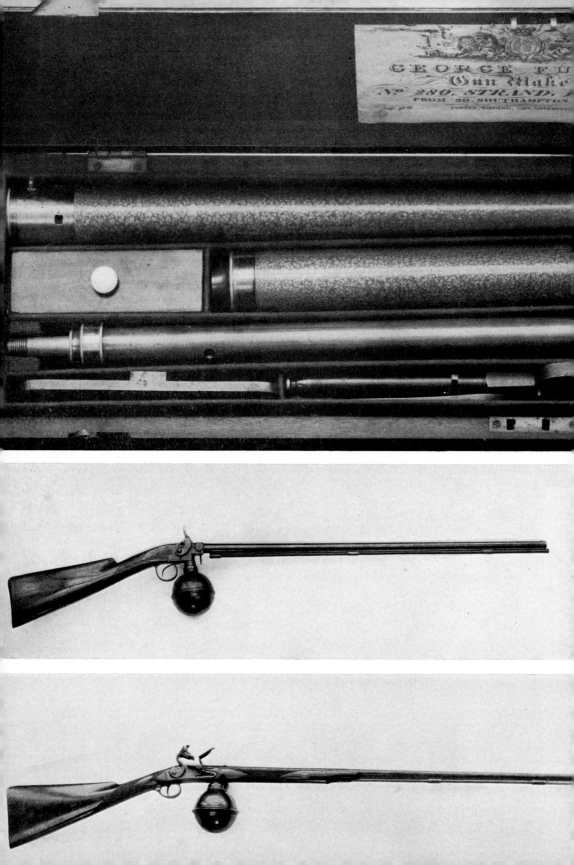

An 'Improved Air Cane' – a walking-stick air
gun with interchangeable smooth and rifled
barrels cased by Fuller of London. It is complete
with pump, bullet mould, cocking key and other
accessories. You look at a formidable weapon which
under a pressure of 400 pounds per square inch,
will penetrate an inch-thick plank of wood at 50
yards fifteen times over at one pumping. For a
collector, Leslie Wesley recalls that he acquired 400
airguns and 280 air pistols without reaching
a definitive selection.

pneumatic arms air storage containers are variously
sposed, but, commonly, in a hollow metal ball as in the
m by Beckwith (*top left*). Air guns had such a notorious
pute as the weapons of poachers and criminals that many
ere disguised (*bottom left*) to look and sound like
nventional flintguns. In this weapon by Bate of London,
e cock acts as a lever to the airgun action. But the
wder charge, since there is no connection between the
rrel and the primer, is a deception.

In the list of the great gameshots at the turn of
the century Lord de Grey (later Marquis of Ripon) is always
named first. He was certainly one of the outstanding
performers of the new school of shooting which came into
being with efficiency of design in the mechanism of breech
loading weapons. Colonel Hawker, to make a bag with his
flintlock, had to ride down his birds on horseback until
they were almost too tired to fly. De Grey belonged to
the generation in which, with quick-firing weapons, driven
game shooting was developed – the sport in which the birds
are flushed over the guns as tall and difficult to shoot as
the lie of the country and the skill of the beaters can make
them fly.

The mass rearing of pheasants came about in the late
nineteenth century when shooting with a pair of double-barrelled
guns, and a loader, raised the sport from pot-hunting to an
athletic exercise. De Grey was one of the first masters of it.
The period may be viewed with regret for the slaughter
of animals that it entertained; or with respect for the
physical prowess of shooting men who could fire 20,000 rounds
a season; have three dead pheasants in the air at the same
time; kill two partridges in front, change guns, and drop
two behind. De Grey, who gave up keeping a detailed list
of the game he killed after 1913, bagged between 1867–95
316,699 head including 111,190 pheasants, 89,491 partridges,
47,468 grouse. Up to his death he brought his total
score to well over half a million.

92

The gun by Purdey (*below*) is one of a pair that
de Grey used. It was discovered in useless condition by
Purdey's themselves. They glued the frail tired old arm
together. For the collector, here's the beauty of the
best of the old hammers. With their long lean actions,
they have the lines of a racehorse; a grace which even
the best of the hammerless guns (in which the hammers,
still there, are incorporated under the lock plates) cannot attain.

(*Above*) A 16-bore double-barrelled flintlock gun by James
Purdey the first, built in 1816. Still in mint condition,
it is one of only about a hundred flintguns that Purdey made.
(*Below*) One of a pair of Purdey hammerguns built for Lord de Grey
(Marquis of Ripon) in 1867 (see pages 92–93).
It is noteworthy how much the characteristic stocks of modern
hammerless gameguns owe to the roach-bellied shapes favoured in
muzzleloaders, and later in hammerguns, during the nineteenth century.
The leather cheekpad on the stock of the flintlock was a fashionable
refinement of the time. It fell into disuse as shooters
learnt smoother and more rhythmic gunmounting. Lord de Grey,
in company with other Victorian gameshots, disdained it.

ACKNOWLEDGMENTS

To Mr. W. Keith Neal for specimens from his collection on pages
41, 46, 47, 48, 56, 57; to Mr. Ian Crudlington for specimens on pages
60, 61, 62, 64, 65; to Mr. Harry Lawrence of Messrs. James Purdey &
Sons for specimens on pages 50, 51, 52, 63, 76, 93, 94–95 and the port-
rait of the Marquis of Ripon, which hangs in Purdey's Long Room, on
page 92. To Mr. John Bell for the gun accessories on pages 15, 54,
66–75, 79–85; to Mr. Douglas Fryer and Messrs. Wallis & Wallis, the
auctioneers of Lewes, for the photographs of arms which have passed
through their saleroom, and which are shown on pages 31, 49, 54, 58,
59, 77, 86, 87, 88, 89, 90, 91. To Mr. John Gay for the photos of the
author firing a muzzleloader on pages 8–9. To these gentlemen I am
also indebted for expert advice. If I have nodded, it's no fault of their's.

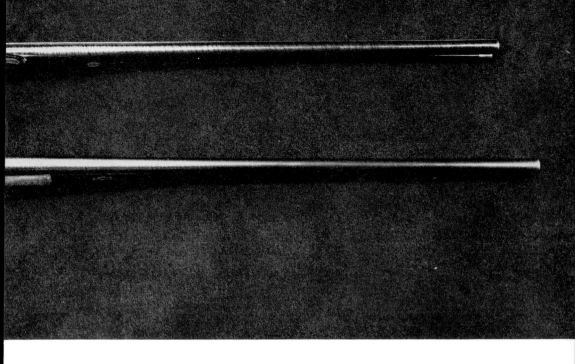

Index

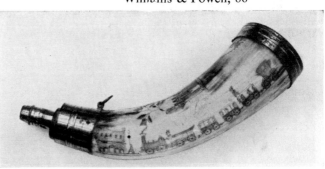

Powder horn decorated with motif of early railway train.